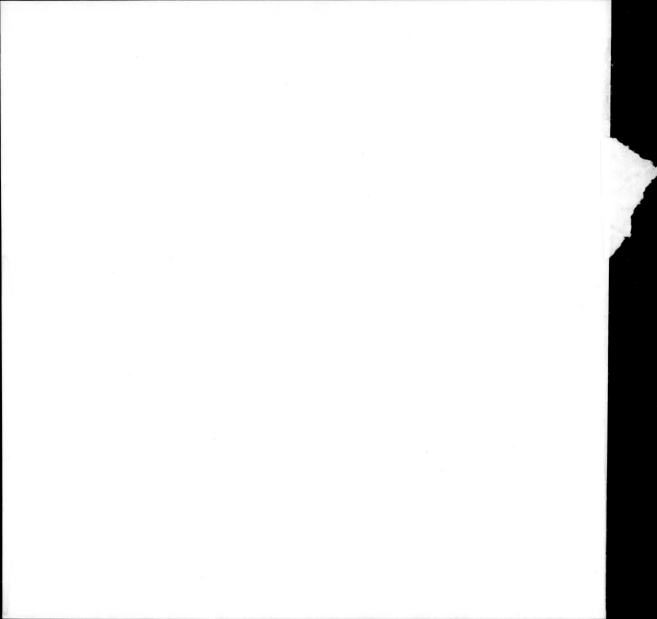

Chakras

Thorsons First Directions

Chakras

Naomi Ozaniec

Thorsons
An Imprint of HarperCollins*Publishers*
77–85 Fulham Palace Road,
Hammersmith, London W6 8JB

The Thorsons website is: www.thorsons.com

Published by Thorsons 2001

10 9 8 7 6 5 4 3 2 1

Text derived from *The Elements of Chakras*, published by Element 1996

Editor: Rachel Harrison
Design: Wheelhouse Creative
Production: Melanie Vandevelde
Photography from PhotoDisc Europe

A catalogue record for this book
is available from the British Library

ISBN 0 0071 2354 X

Printed and bound in Hong Kong

Contents

Chakras

The chakras are centres of living energy that

exist within us all

What are the Chakras?

A chakra is an energy centre within us. 'Chakra' is a Sanskrit word meaning 'wheel'. Just as a wheel spins slowly or rapidly, so a chakra can be more or less active in relation to the degree of energy in a person's system. The wheel itself is a powerful symbol representing the many cyclic patterns of life.

Chakras are also called 'lotuses'. The lotus flower has come to represent the human condition. The flower blooms upon the water, but its roots are deeply buried in the mud far below the surface. Just like a lotus, the chakra can be closed, in bud, opening, or blossoming.

We find teachings concerning the chakras in many major spiritual traditions, including Tibetan Buddhism, Taoist yoga and the western alchemical tradition. Most notable are the Upanishads (Hindu scriptures).

Where are the chakras, wheels or lotuses? They are to be found within each of us. Just as everyone has a physical body, so too does everyone have a **subtle body**. The chakras serve as a bridging mechanism between the physical and the subtle level.

The chakras function as transmuters of energy from one level to another, distributing **prana**, the universal life force that permeates all living things, to the physical body.

By working with the chakras and awakening each in turn, it is possible to regulate the flow of life energy in the body.

Subtle and physical anatomy

The chakras themselves are part of a greater network of subtle energies. Our approach to them must be holistic.

   The six chakras of awakening are equivalent to the body's major systems: cognition, respiration, circulation, digestion, reproduction and excretion. The brain has an additional centre, giving a total of seven major chakras. Each chakra corresponds to certain physical systems and the related organs and glands, as the chart on the right shows.

CHAKRA	ORGAN	GLAND
Muladhara (Base)	large intestine, rectum, kidneys	adrenal
Svadisthana (Sacral)	reproductive system, bladder, kidneys	testes, ovaries
Manipura (Solar Plexus)	liver, gall bladder, stomach, spleen, small intestine	pancreas
Anahata (Heart)	heart, arms	thymus
Vishuddi (Throat)	lungs, throat	thyroid, parathyroid
Ajna (Brow)	brain	pituitary
Sahasrara (Crown)	whole being	pineal

There is a direct relationship between the condition of the chakra and the corresponding physical organs. Physical symptoms will be mirrored by dysfunction within the related energy network and the chakra itself.

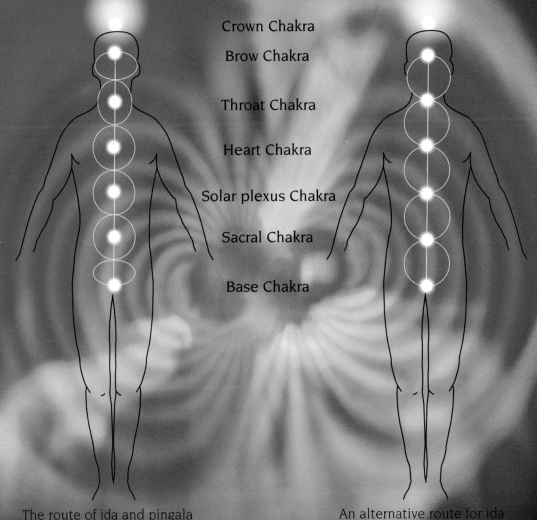

Crown Chakra

Brow Chakra

Throat Chakra

Heart Chakra

Solar plexus Chakra

Sacral Chakra

Base Chakra

The route of ida and pingala

An alternative route for ida
and pingala

The sushumna, ida and pingala meridians

Just as the physical body is far more than a mere collection of organs, the subtle body is far more than a collection of chakras. There is a network of interconnecting energy channels called **meridians**.

The spine is vital in the circulation of subtle energies. The **sushumna**, the most important of the meridians, rises within the base chakra following the spine, and is said to be composed of the forces of life, consciousness and creativity. The chakras are strung upon the inner column of sushumna like jewels on a necklace. It is this central column which unifies the separated chakras into a whole.

There are two other important meridians: **ida** and **pingala**. They emerge from opposite sides of the base chakra and criss-cross up the body, meeting at the brow centre (as shown in the diagram on the left).

Kundalini is the latent power, said to resemble a coiled serpent in form, which lies dormant within the base chakra. When the latent power awakens, the ensuing experience takes many forms. The full awakening of Kundalini brings enlightenment.

The aura

The physical body is surrounded by an emanation called the **aura**. It is made up of the following different bands of energy, which each reflect an aspect of being.

The etheric field/body: the inner layer of the aura is a non-physical luminescence generated by living cells. Patterns of disease appear first within the etheric field.

Discover the etheric field by positioning your hands so that they are facing but not touching each other. Begin to move your hands slowly in and out from each other in a bouncing movement. When the two palm centres interact you will feel what can best be described as a magnetic force between your hands.

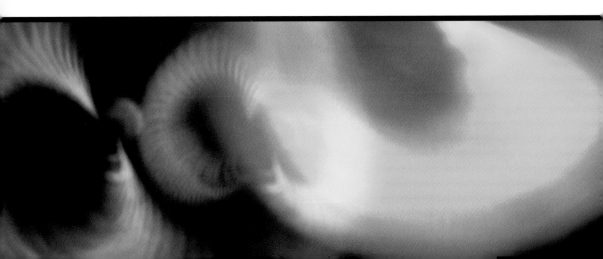

The astral field/body: the middle layer of the aura reflects the emotional nature, and is like a system of personal antennae, which pick up feelings about people and situations. Each human emotion generates a different pattern of energy. The astral field reflects the interplay of emotions like a mirror.

The mental field: the outer layer of the aura. This band of energy reflects the mental nature and develops when the mind is used in certain ways. With the development of the higher mental faculties, the ability to receive inspirational thoughts and intuitive ideas is enhanced.

Working with the subtle energies

The subtle levels of our being indicate hidden levels of potential within us all. We each possess seven major centres of awakening, but many of us have not yet explored the potential that these represent. Our condition can be likened to a person who sits motionless, having yet to discover the functions of their physical limbs.

The chakras can be seen as a series of locked gates, which need to be opened one by one if we are to achieve change. The key we need to open the gates cannot be given to us by anyone, but has to be personally constructed. This key can take many forms, for example applied energy, meditation or physical stimulus.

Approaching the Gates

Once commitment has been made to awakening the chakras, the student must be aware of the following requirements.

Motives: There has to be a genuine commitment to self-discovery and realisation. Anything less will be insufficient to sustain the individual through the inevitable trials and difficulties of the path.

Character building: We must consciously seek to redress any obvious imbalances in the forces that dominate our lives. The five aspects of **Yama** (abstention from evil conduct) must be followed: non-violence, truthfulness, abstention from sex during certain periods, non-stealing and non-greed. The five aspects of **Niyama** (virtuous conduct) must also be adhered to: purification, contentment, asceticism, the recitation of sacred sounds, and the worship of divine beings. Yama and Niyama together prepare the mind for enlightenment, just as the ground is prepared in readiness for the seed.

Commitment to the principle of service: It is important that we should genuinely wish to pass on the benefits of our awakening to others in some way. Right motivation will naturally lead to a commitment to service. Wrong motivation will create the desire to wield power rather than to offer service.

The traditional methods for awakening the subtle energies are meditation, physical postures and breath control. Combined with intellectual study, which provides an overall understanding of the names, locations, functions and inter-relationships of the chakras, these methods constitute an integrated approach to working with the centres.

Meditation

Meditation is a primary tool in all areas of spiritual awakening and is essential for chakra awakening, which cannot safely take place without the states of mind implicit in meditation. The many symbols and qualities of the chakras are used as focal points for meditative practice.

Physical postures

The neck lock
1. Sit with a straight back. Place your palms on your knees.
2. Inhale deeply and hold your breath.
3. Bend your head forwards. Pull in your chin and contract your neck. Pull your shoulders up so that your head is resting on the shoulder muscles. Straighten your arms and lock the elbows.
4. Keep your head centred and lock the posture. Retain the breath comfortably. Exhale and release the lock. Repeat three times.

The diaphragm lock
1. Sit with a straight back. Place your palms on your knees.
2. Exhale deeply, emptying your abdomen and chest.
3. Lift your diaphragm. Pull the upper abdomen up and back.
4. Lock the posture. Hold while it is comfortable. Release and inhale.

The root lock

1.Sit with a straight back. Place your hands on your knees.
2.Exhale deeply. Contract the muscles of your perineum and draw
   them upwards.
3.Draw in the lower abdomen towards the spine.
4.Hold the lock while it is comfortable. Release and inhale. Repeat.

Breathing

The subtle energies are highly responsive to controlled breathing
(**pranayama**). Prana can be directed by regulated breathing under the
control of specific visualisation. Different breathing patterns create
different effects upon the subtle energies.

   These breathing exercises should not be practised on a full stomach or
bladder and should take place in a well-ventilated room. If you can, sit
in the classic lotus position; otherwise, sit so that the spine is straight.

Yogic breathing

1.Inhale deeply.
2.Let the air fill your abdomen. Feel your abdomen expand.
3.Let the air fill your chest area. Feel your rib cage expand.
4.Let the air move into your throat and nasal passages.
5.On exhalation, empty your nasal passages first, then your chest, finally
   your abdomen.

Psychic breathing

This is a very quiet and gentle breath. It may be practised for long periods in conjunction with meditation techniques. It produces a calming effect on the nervous system.

1. Close the glottis at the back of your throat.
2. Breathe deeply and softly. This produces a slight snoring sound.

Here is a technique which combines breath control and visualisation, to help you become attuned to the flow of prana.

Circulation of light

1. Sit with a straight spine.
2. Imagine a reservoir or pool of light at the base of your spine.
3. Inhale slowly and deeply (use the psychic breath). As you do so, draw energy in the form of light up from the base chakra. Let it rise up through the sushumna to the top of your head. When it reaches the top of the head see a cascade of light fountaining out through the head.
4. Let this light circulate on either side of your body and be drawn in again at the base chakra.

This completes one cycle. Perform five cycles.

Chakras and health

The chakras are excellent indicators of well-being. When a chakra is blocked or closed, the individual is no longer able to access the corresponding energies. Imbalance at one level is reflected by imbalance at another. We can therefore use the chakras as a means of diagnosis.

We can locate points in the hands and feet that correspond to the chakras. For example, the reflex points for the pituitary gland (assigned to the brow chakra) are located on the thumbs and big toes. A skilled practitioner can use these points both for diagnosis and as part of treatment.

Try the following to test the relative strengths of the chakras: connect the tip of your right index finger to the tip of your right thumb. Place your left hand over the chakras one at a time. The tester tries to pull your thumb and finger apart. If a chakra is weak, you will not be able to hold out against the pressure from your friend. It is especially helpful to apply this test to assess the strength of a chakra when you are unwell.

The chakras are also highly responsive to approaches that work specifically upon the subtle energies, such as the Bach flower remedies. The right remedy can have an extraordinarily liberating effect upon a blocked chakra.

Awakening chakras

Here are some more techniques to help awaken the chakras.

1. Dreaming can be a vehicle for chakra awakening. Try to incubate a dream by spending the time before sleeping immersed in relevant images and thoughts. Try to recall your dream images as you wake.
2. Positive affirmations can be used like a meditation while you are working with one chakra. Here are some suggestions; alternatively you can make up your own.

    Base chakra: I am a part of the living universe. I acknowledge my connections with all living beings.
    Sacral chakra: I have the power to create. I am able to bring something new into this life.

Solar plexus chakra: I am in control of my own power. I am able to make my own decisions.
Heart chakra: I feel compassion for all living beings.
Throat chakra: I express my deepest thoughts and feelings with clarity.
Brow chakra: I am in tune with an infinite source of guidance.
Crown chakra: I am that I am.

3. Allow the inner mind to provide symbols and images for each of the chakras and draw the images that come to mind as you attune yourself to each of the chakras in turn.

Do experiment with the approaches suggested, but if you experience dramatic results that make you feel unstable or off-balance, stop! Try to rest and allow the energies to stabilise.

The Keys to the Chakras

Each chakra has a symbolic description, which can be thought of as a shorthand or code that summarises the essential qualities of the chakra.

The chakras are allocated to colours, geometric shapes (**yantras**), sounds (**mantras**), elements, animal symbols and presiding deities. Each chakra is described as having a particular number of petals. Sanskrit letters are allocated to each of the chakras.

The chakra images convey little if you just look at them. However, if you internalise the forms through meditation, you will understand not merely the appearance but the meaning of each of the symbolic representations.

Let us now look at the traditional symbols.

The chakras: colours

The chakras are assigned to the colours of the rainbow: red, orange, yellow, green, blue, indigo and violet. This does not mean that the chakras themselves are these colours; the colours indicate the relative vibration of the chakras (moving from the slowest at the base to the most rapid at the top of the head) and represent an attempt to convey the qualities associated with the chakras.

The colours themselves carry certain symbolic values: red is strong and forceful; orange is less aggressive but nevertheless fiery; yellow is solar and warming; green is cool and promotes natural growth; blue is the colour of healing; indigo is expansive; violet is associated with spiritual aspiration.

The petals, yantras and letters of the traditional chakra symbols are also coloured according to a specific code, shown in the table on the right.

CHAKRA	PETALS	YANTRA	LETTERS
Base	crimson	yellow square	gold
Sacral	vermilion	white crescent moon	lightning
Solar plexus	blue-green	red triangle	blue
Heart	vermilion	smoky green hexagon	vermilion
Throat	bright blue	circle in a white triangle	red
Brow	white	golden triangle	white
Crown	not described	not described	not described

The chakras: presiding deities

All but one of the chakras is assigned to a pair of ruling deities, one male, one female (the brow chakra's deity is androgynous). The deities carry items symbolising the lessons that the chakra holds. These symbols can be used as focal points in meditation.

CHAKRA	DEITIES	SYMBOLIC OBJECTS
Base	Brahma	**staff**: channel through which Kundalini rises
		gourd: cup to slake spiritual thirst
		rosary: beads represent names of the Divine Mother
	Dakini	**spear**: need to achieve own targets
		sword: power of discrimination
		staff: empty mind
		cup: waters of life
Sacral	Vishnu	**conch**: need for attentive listening
		disc: concentration
		mace: need to subdue the ego
		lotus: the spiritual goal itself
	Rakini	**trident**: essential unity of mind, body and spirit
		drum: beats out the rhythm of life
		battleaxe: struggle to overcome the negative aspects of self

		lotus: reminder that victory is possible for everyone
Solar plexus	Rudra	**rosary**: transforming emotion into devotion
		fire weapon: the driving power of the emotional life
	Lakini	**thunderbolt**: latent potential energy
		fire weapon: the consuming nature of strong emotion
Heart	Isa	Holds nothing.
	Kakini	**noose**: reminds us not to become captured in the expectation of spiritual experience
		skull: need to maintain a pure mind
Throat	Sadasiva	**noose**: warns against being caught in spiritual pride
		goad: shows further effort is still required
		snake: wisdom
		trident: unity of the physical, etheric and causal bodies
		flame: fires of Kundalini
		bell: inner hearing
		sceptre: indestructibility
		sword: discrimination
		battleaxe: cuts away the old aspects of self
	Sakini (aspect of Gauri)	**bow and arrow**
		noose: don't get caught up in the fascination of sound
		goad: effort still needed
Brow	Sakti Hakini	**drum**: pulse of life
		skull: empty mind
		rosary: held by the student while mantras are recited
		book: wisdom

The chakras: elements

Each of the chakras, except the brow and crown, is also assigned to an element, each of which has particular qualities.

CHAKRA	ELEMENT	QUALITIES
Base	Earth	practicality, survival organisation, structure slow to change; fertile, but requires labour
Sacral	Water	reflection, movement flow, depth cleanses and revives, essence of life
Solar plexus	Fire	action (though needs constant refuelling) change, passion expansion and volatility, warms and comforts has power to change things
Heart	Air	pervasion, omnipresence invisibility, never still can only be seen through its effect unlimited, shared by all
Throat	Akasa	also called 'ether' or 'spirit' refers to eternal undying qualities underlying all manifest forms beyond space and time, a mystery

The chakras: mantras

The **mantra** is a sounded meditation that resonates with the vibration of the chakra. Each chakra is assigned to a different seed sound. Starting at the base chakra these are Lam, Vam, Ram, Yam, Ham and Om. There is no seed sound for the crown chakra.

The chakras: animals

The functions of the chakras are additionally symbolised by various animals. These animal symbols underline the elemental correspondences and also carry the mantra for each chakra.

These are the keys to the chakras, which we will now look at individually.

The Gateway of Earth

The base chakra: table of correspondences

Location	Perineum, between the anus and the genitals
Sanskrit name	Muladhara, from words for 'root' and 'base'/'support'
Element	Earth
Function	Survival, grounding
Inner state	Stability
Body parts	Legs, feet, bones, large intestine, rectum, kidneys
Glands	Adrenals
Malfunction	Obesity, haemorrhoids, constipation, sciatica
Colour	Red
Seed sound	Lam
Sense	Smell
Petals	Four
Animal symbols	Bull, elephant, ox
Deities	Brahma, Dakini. Also Gaia, Demeter, Persephone, Erishkagel, Ana, Ceres, Ceridwen, Geb, Hades, Pwyll

Our journey begins here at the base chakra. The function of this centre is to provide a powerful anchor that links us with all living things.

The base chakra primarily represents our most primitive instincts and the will to survive. It is not surprising that the glands associated with this chakra are the adrenals, which are responsible for the primitive fight or flight response through the output of adrenalin.

Red – the colour of life blood, symbolising the passions and the life force itself – is attributed to this chakra. The colour red is assigned to the planet Mars, which symbolises dynamic, energetic and even aggressive forces. It corresponds well to the qualities and functions of the base chakra.

The dormant, transformative power of Kundalini rests within the base chakra. The complete rising of this force is said to bring liberation and enlightenment. When the power is awakened, it rises up through the chakras and transforms all in its path. **Shakti**, the feminine force, is assigned to the base chakra; **Shiva**, the masculine force, is assigned to the crown chakra. When the two are separated a state of duality prevails. When Kundalini rises fully, Shiva and Shakti unite. Cosmic consciousness is born from their union.

Base chakra: symbol

The traditional Hindu symbol for this chakra has four petals, each inscribed with a Sanskrit letter in gold. The yantra for this chakra is a yellow square; the yantra of earth, representing the stability of physical manifestation. The arrows represent the myriad directions which are ever open to the individual at the physical level. Within the square there is a white elephant with seven trunks, representing the seven minerals necessary for physical life. The elephant is wearing a black collar to indicate servitude.

The inverted triangle represents Shakti, the feminine aspect of creation. Kundalini is represented in the symbol by the serpent wound around the phallus.

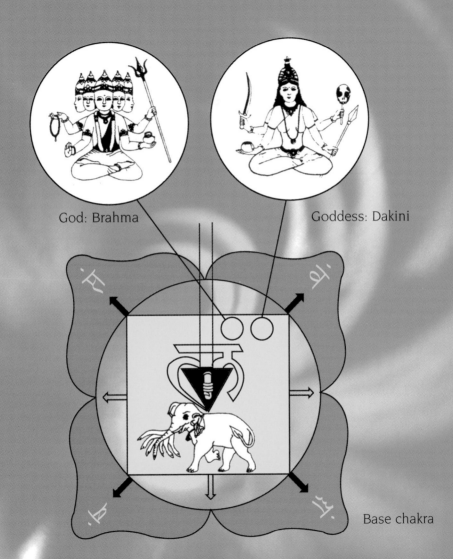

God: Brahma

Goddess: Dakini

Base chakra

Hindu teachings tell us that the base chakra contains a **psychic knot**. These knots, also found at the heart and brow chakras, have to be dissolved to allow the evolutionary energies to flow upwards, creating a state of unity.

In the physical body, this chakra rules the legs and feet, the bones and the large intestine. Imbalances at this level can bring about obesity, sciatica, haemorrhoids, constipation and, in men, prostate problems. Imbalance at this level can also create psychological problems such as conditions of grief, depression and instability. Individuals with these difficulties would benefit from working with the energies of the base chakra.

When the base chakra is active and balanced there is a sense of purpose, a sense of belonging to the natural world and a willingness to take personal responsibility for actions and deeds.

Orientation exercises

These exercises will help you focus on the base chakra.

1. Choose an earth deity. Study their mythology and familiarise yourself with the forms in which they have been represented.
2. Explore your own relationship with the natural world by considering what the earth gives you and what you give the earth.
3. Meditate on the element of earth.

Asanas

Body drops

1. Sit on the floor with legs stretched out in front of you.
2. Support yourself by placing your hands on the floor behind you.
3. Arch your buttocks and bounce gently on the base of the spine.

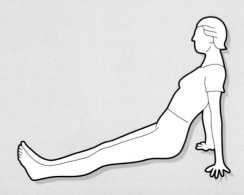

Visualisation: the four horizons

Try the following visualisation to help you work on the base chakra.

See before you a circle traced on the ground, with the four directions clearly marked. In the circle stands a robed figure – your chosen earth deity. The figure invites you to stand in the centre of the circle and points towards the distant eastern horizon.

You find yourself watching a group of men hunting a great animal on foot, armed only with spears and sticks. You run beside them. They work together to bring down the giant beast. You feel a flush of adrenalin, terror mingled with excitement, exuberance combined with concentration. Your legs seem to give way as if you too had participated in the chase and the kill.

The scene fades and you return to the centre of the circle. The deity points towards the next horizon. You find yourself in the thick of a merciless battle. You hear the sound of horses in pain and the distant cries of wounded men. You do not wait to see the outcome of the day for you cannot know if the victor has a just cause. You turn away. The scene fades and you return to the circle.

The deity points to the next direction. You are standing at a city gate, at the foot of a steep, cobbled street. All around are ragged people lying hunched and motionless. At the top of the street is a square, bedecked with flags. The rulers of the city enter in a procession, a blaze of colour. The scene fades and you return to the circle.

The deity points to the last quarter. You are transported to a small hillside overlooking a paddy field, where women are planting rice. They work slowly, patiently, methodically moving through the field in a subtle rhythm. You hope that their harvest will be a good one. The scene fades and you return to the circle.

The deity says, 'You have watched others; how will you use the powers of the earth?' Take time to reflect. The scene finally fades.

Dream images

Work on the chakras can spontaneously produce a wide range of dream images, indicating that an awakening has taken place. When working on the base chakra you may experience dreams that take place underground and reveal a hitherto untapped source of power, possibly in a subterranean chamber, basement or cellar; dreams of underground fire; dreams of opening a hidden trap door; dreams that feature digging for hidden treasure or unearthing items of significance. Dreams featuring a serpent, bull, elephant or other massive beast also relate to this level of consciousness.

Bach flower remedies

Cherry plum	Learning to let go
Clematis	Grounding
Gorse	Integration of joy and sorrow
Pine	Taking responsibility for your own life
Sweet chestnut	Trusting your own development

Music

This chakra responds to earthy tribal music and primitive natural rhythms. The authentic sounds of drumming or chanting may encourage you to dance, stamp your feet or jump. Suggested pieces are *Meetings with Remarkable Alloys* by Chris Campbell or *Spirit of the Red Man* by John Richardson.

The Gateway of the Moon

The sacral chakra: table of correspondences

Location	The sacral plexus
Sanskrit name	Svadisthana, meaning 'sweetness' or 'one's own abode'
Element	Water
Function	Pleasure, sexuality, procreation, creativity
Inner state	Self-confidence, well-being
Body parts	Womb, kidneys, reproductive system, circulation system, bladder, kidneys
Glands	Ovaries, testes
Malfunction	Impotence, frigidity, uterine, bladder or kidney trouble
Colour	Orange
Seed sound	Vam
Sense	Taste
Petals	Six
Animal symbols	Makara (a crocodile-like creature), fish, sea creatures
Deities	Vishnu, Rakini

Rising up from the base chakra, we now encounter the sacral chakra.

This chakra is located within the abdomen, midway between the pubic bone and the navel. It governs sexuality, procreation and creativity at all levels.

Physically, this chakra affects the flow of fluids in the body – blood, urine, menstrual flow and seminal fluids. Its element, not surprisingly, is water. Water carries a deeply symbolic value within many major spiritual traditions. It symbolises purification and represents birth consciously undertaken.

The fact that this chakra is allied to sexuality is significant. The personal sexual union symbolises the cosmic union, the meeting of male and female polarities. In awakening the chakras, we are aiming for just such a unity. Just as the intensity of sexual encounter can sometimes transcend the physical confines of the experience, so can a higher level of experience be attained by awakening the chakras.

Traditionally, it is thought that there is a direct link between this chakra and the mind. The life energies that are generated here circulate upwards into the higher chakras, like a rising head of steam. The sacral chakra has to be cleared of karmic debris before Kundalini can rise any higher. Hence frustration, both sexual and creative, can be generated here when the life energies are blocked.

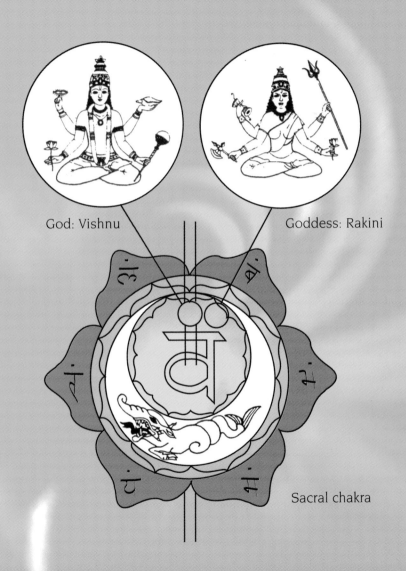

God: Vishnu

Goddess: Rakini

Sacral chakra

Sacral chakra: symbol

The sacral chakra has six vermilion petals. The strong colour indicates that the impulses, ideas and desires generated here are stimulating to the mind.

The yantra for this chakra is a crescent moon. The moon is identified with the hidden unconscious forces; in addition, lunar symbols are traditionally identified with women, whose menstrual rhythms also follow a cyclic pattern. The moon is connected with all waters: the rise of sap, the flow of blood and the movement of the tides.

The sacral chakra's animal symbol is a makara, a crocodile-like creature. The fish or sea-creature is a classic symbol for the deep and turbulent waters of the subconscious or for interaction with the astral world.

When the chakra awakens it brings increased powers of intuition and increasing psychic abilities. The sex drive can be dramatically affected, either positively or negatively. In each case the effects are usually short-lived and stabilise as the energies settle.

When this chakra is balanced it brings a sense of self-confidence and creativity. The imagination is used constructively and sexual energy brings a sense of completeness and integration.

Orientation exercises

1. How do you use the function of sexuality? What meaning does it have for you?
2. Meditate on the element of water.

Asanas

The locust pose

1. Lie on your stomach with your hands beside your thighs with palms down.
2. Stretch and raise your legs with your abdomen as high as possible keeping the knees straight. Hold for a few seconds and then lower to the floor. Repeat up to five times.

The cat–cow pose

This exercise works at points along the spine.

1. Place your hands and knees on the floor, so that you are making a bridge with your back.
2. Inhale, arch the back and raise your head.
3. Exhale, round the back and drop the head downwards. Establish a rhythm of inhaling, head up, and exhaling, head down. Continue this for about one minute.

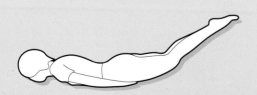

Visualisation: the womb of the mother

Darkness surrounds you, yet the dark feels comforting and safe. You are floating suspended in water, deep in the womb of the one who nurtured you. You move and sway, floating in your bubble. Here there are no thoughts, no fears, just life, growing, changing, developing. You are surrounded by another's life, beyond the waters. This great being surrounds you with her love. Time has no meaning for you but time passes and the waters change.

You grow and are nourished by the waters while nine moons pass. You fill the waters and are finally born from them. Every human being begins in the darkness and the waters. There is no other way of life.

Dream images

This chakra tends to produce dreams in which water images appear. The quality of the water in the dream is indicative of the way in which this chakra is functioning. Stagnant, dirty or foul water requires inner cleansing. Frozen water or ice requires thawing. Images of bathing or washing indicate that a cleansing process has commenced. Swimming indicates ease with the functions of this chakra. Drowning indicates difficulties. Fountains or gushing waters indicate the sudden or unexpected awakening of this chakra. Meetings with water-dwelling creatures indicate that some aspect of this chakra is being integrated.

Dreams involving the moon are also related to this chakra. Travelling to the moon or exploring a lunar landscape indicate inner exploration at this level.

Bach flower remedies

Crab apple	Getting rid of what you cannot digest
Elm	Turning your ideas into reality
Mimulus	Freedom within a structure
Oak	Surrender
Vervain	Accepting others
Wild rose	Taking part joyfully in life

Music

Sensual, flowing music is appropriate here. Traditional music for belly dancing has the power to release the energies of this chakra.

The Gateway of the Sun

The solar plexus chakra: table of correspondences

Location	Rooted between the twelfth thoracic vertebra and first lumbar vertebra
Sanskrit name	Manipura, meaning 'lustrous gem' or 'city of jewels'
Element	Fire
Function	Will, power
Inner state	Intense emotion: laughter, joy, anger
Body parts	Digestive system, liver, spleen, stomach, small intestine
Glands	Pancreas
Malfunction	Ulcers, diabetes, eating disorders such as anorexia and bulimia, hypoglycaemia
Colour	Yellow
Seed sound	Ram
Sense	Sight
Petals	Ten
Animals	Ram
Deities	Rudra, Lakini, Apollo, Agni

We rise up from the fluid sacral chakra to encounter the fire of the solar plexus chakra.

Physically this chakra governs the stomach and digestive system, and relates to the liver, gall bladder and spleen. Imbalances can give rise to eating or digestive disorders. Ulcers, which are frequently related to high levels of stress, are a classic disorder of this centre.

Just as the physical digestive system extracts energy from food, so the solar plexus chakra extracts and stores prana. Prana can be directed to any of the body's systems, or from one person to another, through the power of the directed imagination.

Prana is universal to all living things. Bioenergetic foods – seeds, grains, nuts and pulses – along with fresh vegetables and fruit radiate the life force that is prana. Living food enhances the whole being. A diet built around living food will contribute over a period of time to raising the vibrations of the subtle energies to a higher level.

The solar plexus chakra is a central point at which all things, both visible and invisible, find their balance. When this chakra functions at the gravitational centre of being, emotions are both felt and expressed. When the powers of this centre are repressed, the chakra acts like a dam, holding back feelings, energies, needs and drives. There is inner turmoil, repressed anger. The stomach is very sensitive to sudden changes in our feelings: nervousness produces butterflies in the stomach; a shock can feel like a physical blow. These physical sensations are mirror images of the activity of the chakra itself.

Traditionally, the awakening of this chakra is said to bring the power to locate hidden treasure – this may refer to the treasure that is spiritual reality. An active solar plexus chakra is said to confer mastery over the internal fires and the ability to generate psychic heat. The ability to see the body from within is also said to develop as the functions of this chakra unfold.

God: Rudra

Goddess: Lakini

Solar plexus chakra

Solar plexus chakra: symbol

The traditional image for this chakra has ten petals and is coloured greenish-blue. In the centre is a downward-pointing red triangle, the region of fire, with additional T-shaped projections at each edge to suggest movement.

The element of the solar plexus chakra is fire. The ram, vehicle of Agni, the god of fire, represents the qualities of this chakra. It is interesting to note that Rudra, the male deity, has both a vengeful and a benign aspect, indicating that power can be used both positively and negatively, in much the same way as fire can be. Rudra is known as 'the red one'. He is often depicted as being ruddy in colour, but is also shown with a white face smeared with ashes.

When the energies of this chakra are active and balanced, the individual enjoys well-being and has a clear sense of personal self-determination.

Orientation exercises

1. Explore the concept of personal power by considering how you use power in the world.
2. Meditate on the element of fire.

Asanas

Belly push

1. Sit with your legs outstretched, hands flat on the floor underneath your shoulders.
2. Lift your body by raising your buttocks.
3. Make a straight line with your body from the toes to the head.
4. Drop back to a seated position and repeat.

Spinal flex

This exercise flexes the spine in both directions.

1. Sit on your heels with your hands on your knees and curve your back.
2. Inhale and arch your back. Push your chest up and out.
3. Exhale as you slump down. Repeat the cycle.

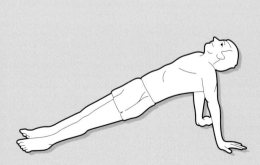

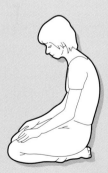

Visualisation: greeting the sun

Picture yourself standing on a high outcrop of rock in a barren, treeless landscape. It is still quite dark; dawn is about to break. Your vantage point enables you to look out across the land – a vast desert plain stretching in every direction. Here and there you see huge stony outcrops like fingers reaching up into the sky. At the distant edge of the horizon, the sun begins to rise. It seems red in colour as it comes into view. You raise your arms in greeting as this great being emerges from the darkness of night. Sunlight begins to flood the terrain, lighting up the seemingly endless vista. You feel a touch of warmth on your face as the sun's rays lengthen.

As the sun rises higher into the sky, changing in colour from red to a burning yellow, it seems to ignite the spark within your own fire centre. Your mind fills with the image of a radiating sphere deep within your centre of being. It glows with brightness that spreads outwards, rising within you as a great fiery ball. You begin to breathe deeply, drinking in the rays of the sun. As you breathe in, you are filled with a shower of brilliance. As you breathe out, you radiate this divine energy towards other living forms.

As you stand in the ever-increasing brightness of a new day, become aware of the living quality of the whole landscape. Everything radiates life. As you continue to breathe deeply, you feel in touch with the very life force of the land, the stones, the sand and the air itself. As you breathe in, you feel that you are drinking in the power of the land, sharing in its daily cycle of renewal. This force fills your power centre, flooding you with vital life force. You feel wholly alive, empowered, exhilarated. Your own energy store is now full to overflowing. Take this power into your life and use it to be fulfilled.

Dream images

Work on this chakra produces dreams with a wide array of
fiery images: setting a fire; preparing a ritual fire; watching
a house on fire; even being on fire but paradoxically being
unharmed, much like the burning bush. Images of sunrise
or other solar images can be indicative of an awakening at
this level.

Bach flower remedies

Aspen	Overcoming fears
Hornbeam	Being able to achieve personal goals
Impatiens	Patience
Larch	Self-awareness
Scleranthus	Balance within yourself
Star of Bethlehem	Ability to act from joy

Music

This chakra is concerned with expressing emotions. Music
that has the power to express an emotion, whether it is
grief or joy, can provide a much-needed cathartic
experience. You might like to listen to **Sunrise** by David
Sun, **The Enchanter** by Tim Wheater and **Aquamarine**
by Stairway.

The Gateway of the Winds

The heart chakra: table of correspondences

Location	Between the fourth and fifth thoracic vertebrae
Sanskrit name	Anahata, meaning 'unstruck'
Element	Air
Function	Love
Inner state	Compassion, love
Body parts	Lungs, heart, arms, hands
Glands	Thymus
Malfunction	Asthma, blood pressure, heart disease, lung disease
Colour	Green
Seed sound	Lam
Sense	Touch
Petals	Twelve
Animal symbols	Antelope, birds, dove
Deities	Isa, Kakini

Rising up from the solar plexus, we now encounter the heart chakra.

The symbolism of the heart as the place of love is obvious, but the form of love assigned to the heart chakra is quite different from personal love. It is universal, unconditional love, a continuous flow of living energy through the heart chakra towards others. This energy has the power to heal and change. If the heart is to be opened in this way, it must be emptied of selfish desires. The model of the selfless, all-loving, all-giving being represents the highest state of individual aspiration.

The element relating to this chakra is air. Practising deeper breathing counteracts the tendency to live in a shallow manner. There is a direct link between the control of the breath and the control of prana.

The heart chakra controls the sense of touch, as the heart meridians run along the length of the arms into the hands. It is through our hands that we offer love in the form of a loving caress or a healing touch. Prana is most easily radiated through the hands, and with appropriate visualisation can be directed from the heart chakra itself.

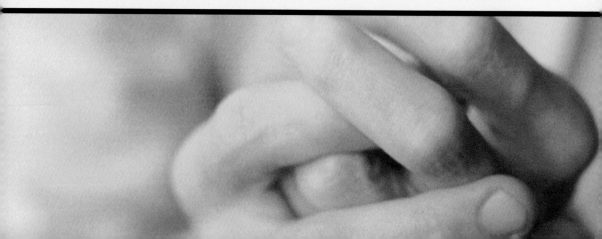

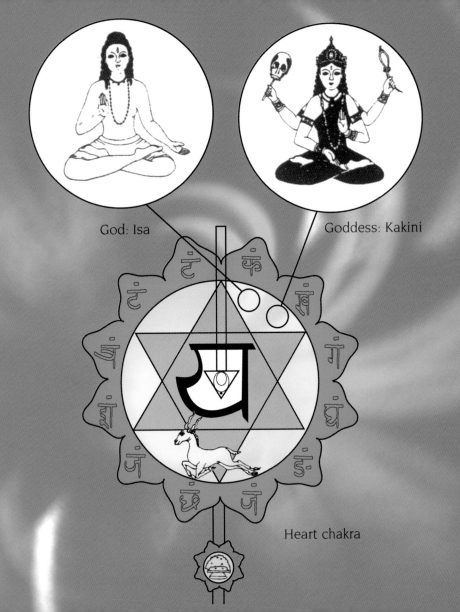

God: Isa

Goddess: Kakini

Heart chakra

Heart chakra: symbol

This chakra is described as having twelve vermilion petals. The yantra is a hexagonal star, composed of the upward-pointing triangle of consciousness and the downward-pointing triangle of force. At the centre of the star is a downward-pointing triangle containing a crescent moon which symbolises the psychic knot in this chakra.

The animal symbol is a black antelope or gazelle, which leaps and bounds with ease, symbolising the lightness of physical substance.

When this centre awakens, the individual becomes highly sensitised to the energy fields of others and is able to detect areas of disturbance and disease. The ability to heal is a natural extension of the increased capacity for love. The power to love impersonally and without discrimination is the central quality of this chakra. In addition, it is said to bring poetic genius and eloquence.

When this chakra is open and balanced there is a genuine ability to give and to receive. Compassion develops and becomes a natural expression of feeling.

Orientation exercises

1. Explore your own experiences of giving and receiving love.
2. Meditate on the element of air.

Asanas

Flapping wings

This exercise helps release constrictions in the chest area. It stimulates the points normally used to treat cardiovascular problems, and counteracts bad posture.

1. Stand with your arms outstretched.
2. Stretch your arms backwards without bending the elbows so that you feel a pressure in your shoulder blades.
3. Keep bending your hands backward.
4. Inhale and raise your chest up and outwards. Exhale. Keeping the arms outstretched bring your palms together in front of you, curving the spine slightly forward.
5. Take your hands back on the inhalation.
6. Bring them forward on the exhalation.

Crossing the heart

1. Sit cross-legged if possible.
2. Place your right hand in the left armpit and your left hand in the right armpit.
3. Close your eyes and feel your heart beating.
4. Attempt to locate the heart space and meditate upon it. A vision of a blue lake and a blue lotus may appear during this pose.

Visualisation: the rose of the heart

Focus your awareness upon the area of the physical heart and its cavity. Try to feel the beating of your own heart. Begin to think of the people that you are able to love. Allow their faces to rise up singly and acknowledge each one individually. Look into the heart space and see the bud of a rose slowly unfolding. Continue to think about the people you love. Now think of those who love you. Watch the rose increasing in size. Allow the rose to complete its growing until it seems to fill your heart. Now let the love you have accumulated stream out from the heart in a shaft of bright light to those whose hearts are empty.

Dream images

Dreams relating to the heart chakra typically involve scenarios in which love is a central theme: being in love, falling in love or even losing love. Such dreams often evoke a keenly-felt emotional response, such as joy or deep sadness.

Bach flower remedies

Centuary	Service
Chicory	Overcoming distance
Heather	Unconditional love
Holly	Free-flowing love energy
Honeysuckle	Living in the here and now
Red chestnut	The ability to express true love
Rock rose	Overcoming ego limitations

Music

Everyone is familiar with certain pieces of music which have the power to melt the heart. The natural sounds of whales and dolphins can take us beyond ourselves. Pachelbel's *Canon* is a wonderfully soothing and healing piece of music. Further suggested pieces are *Great Piece* by Robert Martin, *Quiet Water* by Fitzgerald and Flanagan, *The Response* by John Richardson, *Edge of Dreams* by Phil Thornton and *Deep Enchantment* by David Sun.

The Gateway of Time and Space

The throat chakra: table of correspondences

Location	The throat
Sanskrit name	Vishuddi, meaning 'to purify'
Element	Akasa
Function	Creativity, communication
Inner state	Intuition, synthesis
Body parts	Neck, shoulders, lungs, throat
Glands	Thyroid and parathyroid
Malfunction	Sore throat, swollen glands, colds, thyroid problems
Colour	Bright blue
Seed sound	Ham
Sense	Hearing
Petals	Sixteen
Animals	Elephant
Deities	Sadasiva; Sakini (an aspect of Gauri)

We have now reached the throat chakra.

The throat chakra represents our power to communicate verbally. Speech permits communication of a complex and unique kind, although nowadays we are so surrounded by words that our ability to communicate has become deadened. Discovering the power of effective, genuine communication is one of the possibilities presented by this chakra.

The compelling qualities of sound are reflected in the mantras, either single words or short phrases used much like meditations. The mantra is sounded at the physical level, but it affects the whole being.

The function of hearing is assigned to this chakra; that is, a subtle quality of inner hearing. By tradition, the opening of this chakra brings increased telepathic rapport, which

can be thought of as hearing inwardly.

There is a link between the development of inner hearing and the process of creativity. When the throat chakra is inactive, our creativity will likewise be subdued.

Activation of the throat chakra is said to bring complete indestructibility; not physical indestructibility, but a certain and absolute knowledge that consciousness itself cannot be destroyed or harmed under any circumstances.

Throat chakra: symbol

This chakra is traditionally depicted with sixteen bright blue petals inscribed with vowel sounds. The yantra is a downward-pointing triangle containing a circle, representing the Gateway of Liberation. The element for this chakra is akasa (the fifth element, also called 'ether' or 'spirit').

The animal associated with this chakra is the white elephant, which we first saw at the base chakra wearing a black collar to indicate servitude. Now the collar has been removed and servitude has been transformed into service.

When this chakra is open and balanced, we understand the past, present and future. The powers of communication and creativity come to life, adding a new dimension to our comprehension of experience.

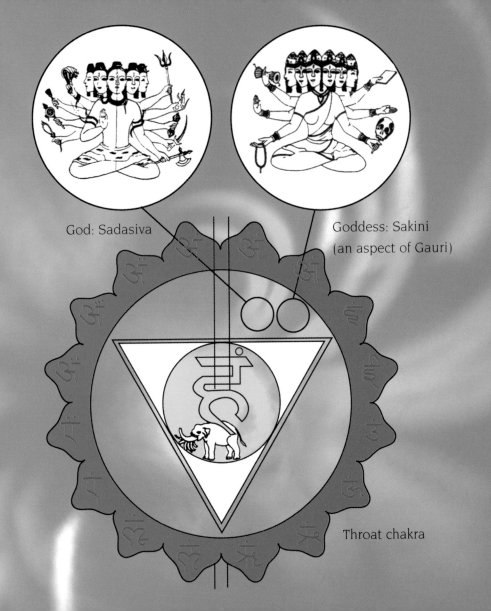

God: Sadasiva

Goddess: Sakini
(an aspect of Gauri)

Throat chakra

Orientation exercises

1. Explore your own powers of communication by reflecting on what you say and how you say it.
2. Meditate on the element of akasa.

Asanas

Bridge

1. Lie comfortably on your back with your legs bent and the bottoms of your feet flat on the floor; keep your hands by your sides.
2. Inhale, bringing your arms up over your head to rest on the floor behind you.
3. Lift your pelvis upwards.
4. Exhale and lower your body down to the starting position.
5. Continue this exercise for one minute.

Bridge

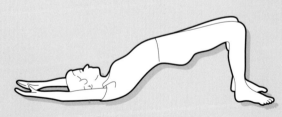

Side to side

This simple exercise opens up the neck and stimulates the thyroid gland.

1. Lie comfortably on your back; inhale deeply.
2. Exhale and slowly turn your head to the left.
3. Inhale as your head returns to the centre.
4. Exhale as you turn your head to the right.
5. Continue this exercise for one minute, gently stretching your neck from side to side.

Visualisation: the womb of space

Imagine that you stand before a great white wall. Step closer and place your hands upon it. You will find that it is light, as if made from a gossamer fabric stretched taut. Feel the soft surface billowing against your hands. Take hold of the substance with both hands. Allow the wish to pass through the veil to rise within you.

The veil opens between your hands, creating a portal. You look beyond the veil and see the darkness and the wonder of deep space lit by points of white light. Decide whether to step back and close the veil or to step out into the unknown. If you wish to carry on, step out with trust. You float in the silence of space, supported by space itself. Surrender to your weightlessness and begin to enjoy the new experience. Bright stars pepper the sky; some seem so close that you feel you could touch them.

As you float, you suddenly and unexpectedly become aware of a sound that seems to come from everywhere at once. It startles you momentarily. Lie back and listen, trying to hear the sound more clearly. It swells in volume and becomes more complex. Now a new sound emerges – the sound of your name. The sound repeats like a mantra. You may answer if you wish, not with your voice but with your mind.

The power of sound carries you along on a wave which rises and falls with the patterns of your name. Your body itself begins to vibrate. Your whole being takes up the resonance; you feel as if the very sound sloughs away the superfluous aspects of your existence.

Ahead of you see the white gossamer veil with the open portal. You are carried gently there, and step through the opening to touch terra firma again. It feels good to return, but it also feels good to have journeyed.

Dream images

Dreams related to the throat chakra most often involve visits to highly unusual, foreign or strange places: mountain tops, hidden lands, undiscovered territories or quite alien landscapes. Contact is often made with a foreign race that appears to be superior in wisdom and understanding. Teaching is often offered, either formally or informally. In the dream the content of this teaching carries great weight, yet paradoxically it seems difficult to recall it upon waking.

Bach flower remedies

Agrimony	Fusing thinking and feeling
Mustard	Trusting yourself even in the face of adversity
Wild oat	Communicating from your deepest levels
Willow	Making space for creativity

Music

The throat chakra expresses both the creativity of the individual and the spaciousness of the group. Immerse yourself in the sound of massed voices, whether choirs or sacred chants. Lose yourself in the whole and find your own note.

The Gateway of Liberation

The brow chakra: table of correspondences

Location	The brow, just above the bridge of the nose
Sanskrit name	Ajna, meaning 'to know', 'to perceive' or 'to command'
Element	None applicable
Function	Direct perception
Inner state	Self-mastery
Body parts	Eyes, two hemispheres of the brain
Gland	Pituitary
Malfunction	Headaches, nightmares, defects of vision
Colour	Indigo
Seed sound	Om
Sense	None applicable
Petals	Two
Animals	None applicable
Deities	Sakti Hakini

We now rise up to the centre commonly associated with the third eye, the brow chakra.

The brow chakra is located at the junction of the ida, pingala and sushumna meridians, and may be thought of as the command centre of the whole being. It is the first of the chakras to have its physical counterpart in the brain rather than in the body. Although there is some debate, the brow chakra is usually attributed to the pituitary gland, which is the body's own command centre for the endocrine system. This chakra holds the last of the psychic knots, which must be dissolved before the Kundalini serpent

can rise fully and awaken the crown chakra.

The awakened brow chakra is the eye of the soul, bringing all-round vision. The activation of this chakra increases the powers of visualisation, the power to see with the mind's eye. When visualisation is allied to everyday thinking, it seems to open the door to new levels of perception and awareness, bringing freedom at many levels.

Brow chakra: symbol

The traditional symbol for this chakra has two petals on either side of a circle. The circle represents the void, beyond time and space; it is not empty, but a state of pure existence. The two petals represent the primal duality which is present in everything. Alternatively, they can be seen as wings: an image of flight, freedom and liberation. The yantra is a downward-pointing golden triangle.

The deity for this chakra is especially interesting. Sakti Hakini is both male and female. It is significant that only one deity represents the powers of this chakra as the ida, pingala and sushumna meridians unite here to create a single current.

The awakening of the brow chakra brings contact with a source of wisdom which is experienced internally, as part of a oneness.

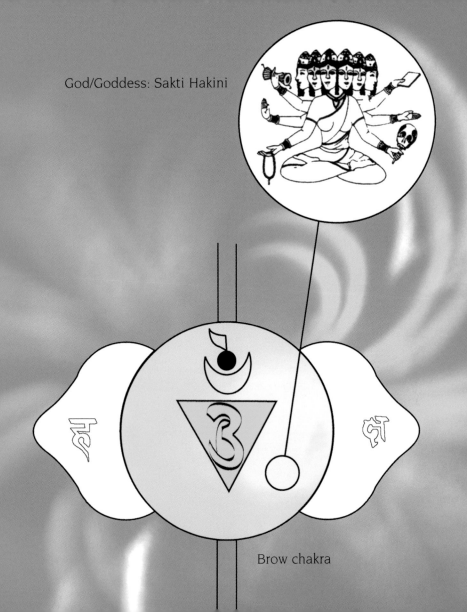

God/Goddess: Sakti Hakini

Brow chakra

Orientation exercises

Try out your ability to visualise. The following exercises are very simple.

1. Sit comfortably, close your eyes and relax. Become aware of the fact that the brain is composed of two hemispheres. Visualise the number '1' in the left hemisphere and the letter 'A' in the right hemisphere. Next visualise '2' in the left hemisphere and 'B' in the right hemisphere. Continue until you reach '26' and 'Z'. Pause and enter deep relaxation. Breathe in and out through the brow chakra.

Now repeat the exercise by placing the letters in the left hemisphere and the numbers in the right. When you have done this you might like to compare the difference.

2. Imagine the sun rising in the right hemisphere and setting in the left. Then imagine the moon rising in the left hemisphere and setting in the right. Relax and allow images that symbolise each of the hemispheres to arise spontaneously.

Asanas

Awakening the eye

1. Sit with your legs crossed so that one heel presses into the area of the perineum.
2. Place your hands on your knees, keeping the spine straight.
3. Concentrate on a point between your eyebrows. Begin alternately to contract and relax your perineum upon inhalation and exhalation.
4. Next, imagine prana being absorbed into the brow chakra on the inhalation. On the exhalation imagine prana as a stream of light being radiated outwards into the universe. Chant the mantra 'Om'.

Clearing the mind

This exercise stimulates the pituitary gland.

1. Sit in a comfortable position with your hands on the floor behind you.
2. Spread your fingers so that you are aware of a slight pressure within your wrists.
3. Bring your head back and begin rhythmic breathing while maintaining awareness of a point between your eyebrows. On the inhalation, imagine that air in the form of white light is coming into the third eye. On the exhalation, imagine it passing out.

Clearing the mind

Visualisation: the place in the clouds

Visualise yourself standing within an open, circular balcony at the top of a high tower. Feel a soft breeze on your face. You look out from your eyrie. Here, you are above the clouds. The sky is bright with an unfamiliar clarity. In the sky hangs a bright sun. You turn your full attention to the world far below, obscured by the clouds. You know that far away, life continues as it always has done.

Now you open the inner senses. In your mind, images arise of people going about their everyday lives in the world below. You watch in your inner mind as familiar scenes pass before you: children play, people sing, girls dance, a group of people raise their voices in worship.

From your vantage point you have total vision. You walk to the other side of your balcony and allow the inner mind to open again. Different sounds greet you; different images fill your mind. Children cry out in pain, mothers weep, young men exult in the sounds of war, old men wail.

Yet here all about you, the air is clear and bright. You are surrounded by great beauty and there is a sense of infinite peace. You want to bring this to the suffering people below.

Perch upon the edge of the balcony and then, when you are ready, leap into the air. Your descent is slow. As you fall, keep reminding yourself of the need to remember what you have seen. As you fall, the light fades and dims, all becomes hazy. There is only silence now, but you know you will find the suffering people. You hope that you have not forgotten what you came to tell them.

Dream images

This level of consciousness transcends the dream state; it is beyond the realm of dreaming.

Bach flower remedies

Beech	Tolerance
Cerato	Following the inner guide
Chesnut bud	Being open to learning from life
Gentian	Acceptance
Olive	Trusting cosmic harmony
Walnut	Being able to listen to the inner voice

Music

Use music to stimulate your natural ability to visualise. Enter a piece of music and allow scenes and images spontaneously to appear in the mind's eye. Try listening to *Freefall* by Malcolm Harrison, *Cascade* by Terry Oldfield or *Inner Harmony* by Arden Wilkin.

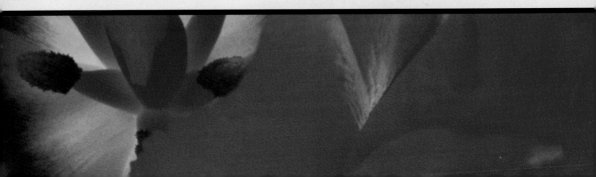

The Gateway of the Void

The crown chakra: table of correspondences

Location	Crown of head
Sanskrit name	Sahasrara, meaning 'thousandfold'
Element	None applicable
Function	Union
Inner state	Bliss
Body parts	Cerebral cortex, brain, the whole body
Gland	Pineal
Malfunction	Alienation
Colour	Violet
Seed sound	None applicable
Sense	None applicable
Petals	One thousand
Animals	The risen serpent
Deities	Shiva

We now reach our destination. We have arrived at the crown chakra and our journey is complete.

The crown chakra is located four finger-breadths above the crown of the head. If you are sensitive, you can feel the presence of this chakra by holding your hand with a flat palm above the top of the head for a few moments. There is a tingling or prickling sensation which emanates from above the head but can also be felt at the top of the head.

The crown chakra is the goal of the risen Kundalini. Once Kundalini has attained this goal, the opposing masculine and feminine forces – Shiva (assigned to the crown chakra) and Shakti (assigned to the base chakra) – are brought together, bringing a state of unity and enlightenment. The level of consciousness represented by the awakened crown chakra is itself the crowning achievement of the human condition.

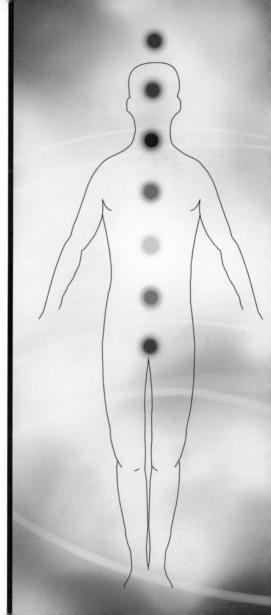

Crown chakra: symbol

This chakra is represented as a multi-layered lotus of a thousand white petals. Each layer is inscribed with fifty Sanskrit letters – the total sound potential of the Sanskrit alphabet. The whole image conveys the idea of wholeness, completion and realisation, symbolising the totality of creation. On the lotus are symbols of the sun and moon. Within the moon symbol is a series of ever smaller symbols, rather like Russian dolls. First is a lightning-like triangle; within this, the Nirvana-Kala, who grants divine knowledge; within this, Shiva and Shakti, the male and female forces united; within this, the void. The void is not a negation, a vacuum or absence of being. Instead it is seen to be the pure ground of being, the root of liberation.

The crown chakra is unique as it has neither a seed sound nor an elemental attribution.

When this centre begins to awaken it can bring unusually sensitive mental states; richer and deeper emotions can be experienced. The physical body becomes healthy. The power of concentration improves, discernment and insight become deeper and more reliable. The ability to take effective action towards the fulfilment of goals increases. Psychic abilities strengthen. A direct relationship between the spiritual world and the mundane world is formed.

Some teachers take the view that no techniques for working with the crown chakra can be given as it is beyond such a mechanical approach. The most important factor in the awakening of the chakra is genuine dedication, which sustains the individual through long-term spiritual practice and brings inner guidance when there is no external teacher.

Orientation exercise

Explore what you understand by enlightenment.

Asanas

Headstand

The headstand is called the king of postures. Begin by working against a wall for support.

1. Make a pad with a folded blanket.
2. Kneel facing the wall. Interlock your fingers and cup your head in your hands.
3. Place your interlocked hands firmly on the blanket. Make sure that your wrists and forearms are strong.
4. Straighten your legs and begin to walk your feet in towards the wall until your shoulders make contact with the wall. Kick up with your feet.

The communion of light

1. Sit with a straight spine.
2. Raise prana from the base chakra up to the crown chakra in a steady stream of light. Do this on a long inhalation breath.
3. Imagine an aperture opening at the top of your head. Let the energy stream out into the universe.
4. Visualise this energy merging with the source of all life in whatever way you conceive this.
5. On the exhalation, absorb prana through the top of your head. Let it descend to the base chakra. Merge this with the pool of prana at the base of your spine by imagining the two forces coalescing into one.
6. Repeat the pattern of inhalation and exhalation.

It is not appropriate to suggest Bach flower remedies or music for this chakra.

We must remember that the crown chakra represents the potential for enlightenment that we all possess. The sevenfold pattern represented by the chakra system is the blueprint for spiritual development. The awakening of the chakras is a process which must be undertaken if the soul is to evolve and find enlightenment.

The Temple of the Lotus

It is important that we have the right attitude to chakra awakening. We should treat our work with reverence and care.

By making chakra awakening the focal point for ritual work, we accord it a special place in our lives.

The preparation and necessary organisation which are required for any ritual serve to focus all the energies upon the purpose of the work.

To prepare a ritual based on one of the chakras, first understand as much about the chakra as possible.

Prepare the traditional representation of the relevant chakra by painting the symbols in the appropriate colours. You might like to represent the deities of the chakra separately with a picture or other symbol.

The following is a suggested framework for working with the base chakra.

Prepare an altar with a red cloth, a candle, the representation of the base chakra, images or symbols for the deities and any other items that will be called upon.

Create a circle. Light the candle and make a statement placing your work under the auspices of the powers you choose to work with.

State your intention clearly: 'We meet to celebrate the powers of earth, to find the roots which intertwine, to establish the foundation which holds us firm.' You might like to open with appropriate music and/or group dancing.

Focus on the relevant correspondences one at a time, to bring out the meaning of each of the qualities of the chakra, for example:

'Here is red, river of life,

Attendant at birth, still at death.

Red for our passions, red for our life,

Roused beyond measure in our struggle to survive.'

You might like to request a blessing from the presiding deities. Ask for whatever you feel you need from this chakra.

Use the seed sound for a period of group chanting. Then move on to a guided meditation or provide a silent time for individual reflection.

Finally, let each participant receive an appropriate gift (a seed, a crystal or a red stone) to encapsulate the individual experience and represent the energies being taken out into the world.

Close the session by offering thanks to any supra-mundane forces that you have called into the circle and extinguish the central candle. 'Our work is done. Let us return to the outer world. Let each depart in peace one with another.'

Asanas for Prana Circulation

This group of asanas is simple, yet invigorating. They stimulate the joints and help to keep prana freely circulating. Source points of energy, related to specific organs, are located near the wrists and ankles. Using these joints will keep energy flowing.

(Reproduced with kind permission from The Theosophical Publishing House.)

1. Lie flat on your back with your arms at your sides, palms upwards; enter a relaxed state.
2. When relaxed and ready, sit on the floor with legs extended. Place your hands palms down on the floor beside your hips and lean slightly backwards. Flex your toes ten times; flex your ankles ten times back and forth; then draw circles in both directions with each of your feet.

3. Place your right ankle on your left thigh. Hold your ankle with your right hand, rotate your foot ten times in each direction. Repeat with your left foot on your right thigh.
4. Raise your right knee and bend it. Clasp your hands under your thigh. Straighten your leg without touching the ground. Repeat ten times with each leg.
5. Place your right foot on your left thigh. Hold your left knee with your left hand and place your right hand on top of your bent knee. Gently move the bent leg up and down. Repeat with the other leg.
6. Place the soles of your feet together and bring the heels as close to your body as possible. Allow the knees to drop as far as they are able.
7. Squat on the floor. Place your palms on your knees and walk while keeping the squatting position.
8. Sit on the floor, legs extended. Extend your arms forward at shoulder height. Clench and unclench the fingers of each hand ten times. Keep your arms extended forwards. Bend your hands back up as far as possible, then down. Repeat ten times.
9. Extend your arms forward. Drop one arm. Make a fist with your other hand. Rotate your wrists ten times in each direction.
10. Extend your arms forward, palms up. Bend both your arms at the elbows and touch your shoulders with your fingertips. Repeat ten times. Then repeat with your arms extended to the sides.
11. Touch your shoulders with your fingertips. Move your elbows in circles in each direction ten times.

In Conclusion

The purpose of this book has been to introduce you to the chakras and to provide some basic procedures which will enable you to experience them for yourself. The discoveries you make about the chakras will also inevitably be discoveries you make about yourself. I wish you well on your voyage of discovery. Don't expect plain sailing all the way. Be thankful for the journey itself; it is better than the monotonous view from the safe harbour.

Glossary

Ajna chakra The brow chakra.

Akasa Spirit, ether, the fifth element.

Anahata chakra The heart chakra.

Asanas The physical postures of yoga.

Astral body (or field) The astral aspect of the aura. The aura's middle layer

Aura The energy field emanated by the living form.

Causal body (or field) The aspect of being that is based in the causal, universal level.

Chakra 'Wheel'; the centres of living energy located within the subtle body.

Etheric body (or field) The inner layer of the aura.

Gauri 'The Eternal'; the great mother; deity of the throat chakra.

Ida The lunar current that starts at the left side of the base chakra and terminates at the right nostril; also called the Ganges River.

Karma	Action; the law of cause and effect that binds consciousness to the Wheel of Rebirth.
Kundalini	The serpent power dormant within the base chakra.
Makara	A crocodile-like creature related to the sacral chakra.
Manipura chakra	The solar plexus chakra.
Meditation	The discipline of controlling the mind in order to bring about a state of liberation.
Mental body (or field)	The mental aspect of the aura. The aura's outer layer.
Meridian	A channel that conducts pranic energies; also called a nadi.
Muladhara chakra	The base chakra.
Nadi	A channel that conducts pranic energies; also called a meridian.
Nirvana	The state of liberation according to the Buddhist tradition.
Niyama	Virtuous conduct, consisting of five practices.
Pingala	The solar current originating at the right side of the base chakra, terminating at the left nostril; also called the Yamuna River.

Prana	The universal life force that permeates all living things.
Pranayama	The practice of controlling the flow of breath.
Sahasrara chakra	The crown chakra.
Sakti/Shakti	The feminine aspect of the divine in manifestation.
Shiva	The masculine aspect of the divine in manifestation.
Sushumna	The spinal meridian identified with the governor vessel.
Svadisthana chakra	The sacral chakra.
Upanishad	Hindu scriptures.
Vishuddi chakra	The throat chakra.
Yama	Abstention from non-virtuous conduct.